Everybody Pees!

Justine Avery Naday Meldova

Fathers pee.

And mothers pee.

Even old, old grandads and grannies pee.

And they pee

a lot.

Every single day.
Just like ALL of us do.

Oh, dogs and cats have to pee.

And every single bird you see.

They pee high up in the trees.

They pee deep down in the sea.

For every reader,
young and old,
who loves a good giggle.
—J.A.

To my mother,
who often bought me
art supplies and always
believed that I would
become a real artist!
—N.M.

Justine Avery is an award-winning author who loves writing stories for all sorts of readers. She was born in America but grew up—and is still growing up—all over the world as a natural explorer with a curiosity for all things. She's jumped out of airplanes, off of very high bridges, and into shark-infested waters—to name a few adventures. And books are her favorite adventures of all.

Naday Meldova is an artist who graduated from art school in Tula, Russia. She's been illustrating for years, and this is her favorite job!

First published 2021 by Suteki Creative

FIRST EDITION

Copyright © 2021 Justine Avery
Illustrated by Naday Meldova
All rights reserved.

In accordance with international copyright law, this publication, in full or in part, may not be scanned, copied, stored in a retrieval system, duplicated, reproduced, uploaded, transmitted, resold, or distributed online or offline—in any form or by any means—without prior, explicit permission of the author.

But *please do*… lend this book freely! It's *yours*—you own it. So, pass it on, trade it in, exchange it with and recommend it to other readers. Books are the very best gifts.

ISBN: 978-1-63882-138-0
ISBN: 978-1-63882-136-6 (ebook)
ISBN: 978-1-63882-139-7 (hardcover)
ISBN: 978-1-63882-141-0 (audio book)

Discover More...

uniquely wonderful, utterly imaginative children's books by Justine Avery

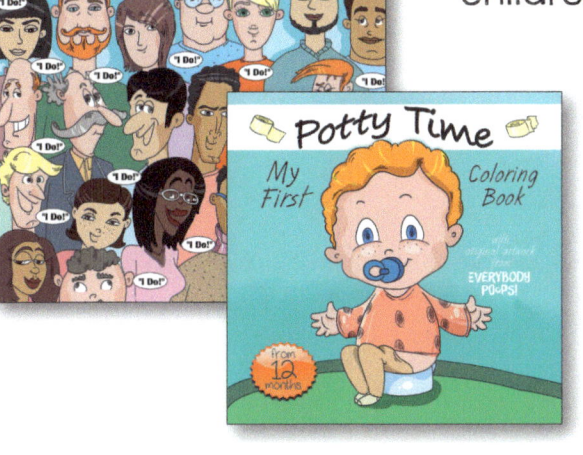

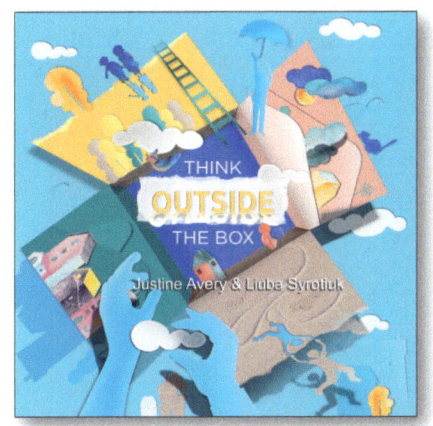

Visit JustineAvery.com and join in the exclusive fun & freebies.

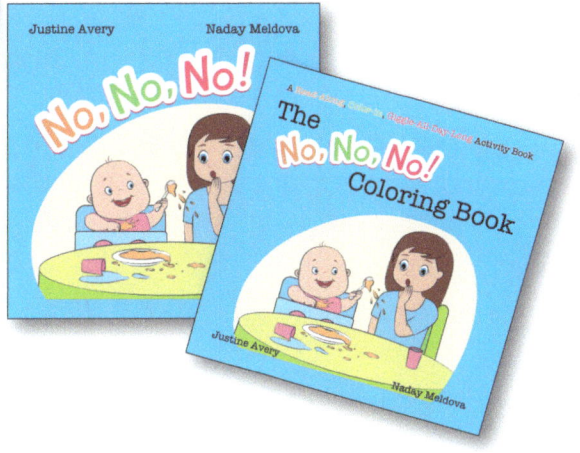

www.ingramcontent.com/pod-product-compliance
Lightning Source LLC
Chambersburg PA
CBHW041108070526
44583CB00002B/106